GROUP DISCUSSION COMPANION

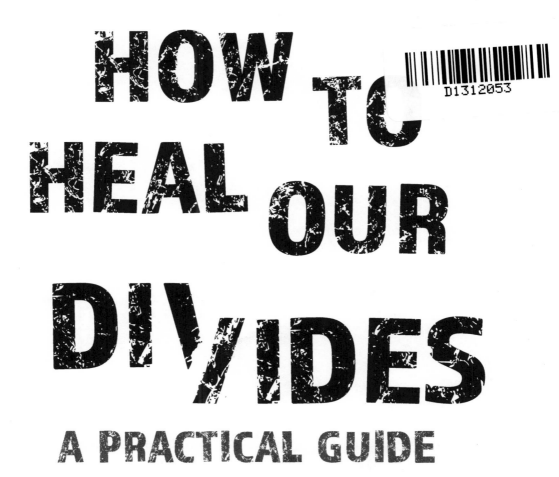

HOW TO HEAL OUR DIVIDES

A PRACTICAL GUIDE

Many thanks to Adam Thomas, Ann Cavera, Nicholas Schaber, and Jennifer Schaber
for their contributions to this Discussion Guide.

To order copies of "How to Heal Our Divides: A Practical Guidebook" (available in Paperback or eBook) visit <u>Amazon</u>, <u>Indiebound</u>, or the <u>Writing for Your Life bookstore on Bookshop</u>.

For additional information on the organizations featured in the book, and the book contributors, please visit <u>www.howtohealourdivides.com</u>.

4 WEEK GROUP DISCUSSION

WEEK 1

CHAPTER 1: "HEALING OUR DIVIDES: WHY THIS MATTERS"
BY BRIAN D. MCLAREN

1. The author describes confirmation bias as: "When a new idea comes along that fits in comfortably with what we already think, our brains welcome it. When a new idea comes along that will upset what we already think, our brains get nervous. The brain realizes it would take a lot of energy to rethink our current assumptions. So it gives us a bad feeling about this new idea… before we are even conscious of it, before we even consider whether it might be true." Describe a time when you may have done this.

2. The author describes complementarity bias as: "If you like me, if you flatter me, if you make me feel good, my brain says, 'Ahhhh. I can use some encouragement from a friendly person.' So I relax and welcome what you say. But if you challenge me, if you appear angry with me, if you don't seem to agree with me and like me, my brain gets nervous. It says, 'This person is going to upset you, and that will take a lot of energy, so I'm just going to give you a bad feeling about them so you won't let yourself be bothered with them.'" Describe a time when you may have done this.

3. The author describes community bias as: "Our brains know that we depend on our belonging groups for security. So our brains monitor our behavior to be sure that we don't get into too much trouble with our belonging groups. If we were to get kicked out, our lives would grow complicated, which would take a lot of energy and threaten our well-being. Our brains monitor our behavior, including what we say and even what we think, and if we are about to think or say something that would get us in trouble with our belonging group, the brain says, 'That's a bad idea. Don't think that. It could get you in trouble.' It gives us a bad feeling about that thought so that we will not need to go find a new belonging group." Describe a time when you may have done this.

4. How much do you think our culture's obsession with sports has influenced us to be "loyal to our side at all costs?"

5. Dr. Martin Luther King said: "The only way to get rid of an enemy permanently is to make him your friend." Is this practical? Who would you consider an enemy that you might be able to make a friend?

REFERENCE READING FOR CHAPTER 1:

*   "Why Don't They Get It? Overcoming Bias in Others (and Yourself)" by Brian McLaren bit.ly/brian-mclaren-book-why

- "The Second Pandemic: Authoritarianism and Your Future" by Brian McLaren
  bit.ly/brian-mclaren-book-authoritarianism

Chapter 5: "Living Into God's Dream: Dismantling Racism in Atlanta and Beyond" by Catherine Meeks

1. What factors enabled the anti-racism commission to lay a firm foundation for the Absalom Jones Center for Racial Healing?
2. How many of these factors does our community already have in place?
3. Assuming that we cannot, and do not want to, mandate participation in training and other forms of racial healing, how can we still foster that participation?
4. For those who do not believe that racism exists or is systemic, and perhaps don't even want to discuss it, how can we help them see and understand it?
5. The Center for Racial Healing partners with local congregations. How can you motivate your local congregation, or other group, to engage with the Center?

Video interview with Catherine Meeks: bit.ly/catherine-meeks-interview

Reference reading for Chapter 5:

- "Living into God's Dream: Dismantling Racism in America" by Catherine Meeks
  bit.ly/catherine-meeks-book

Chapter 13: "3 Practices for Healing Our Divides" by Jim Hancock and Jim Henderson

1. Are there people with whom you want — or need — to stay connected, but honestly-held differences threaten to separate you permanently? What have you done to try to maintain or patch those relationships?
2. Do you know someone you could describe as "unusually interested in others"? What do you think is their secret?
3. Do you know someone you think is particularly good at "staying in the room with difference" How do you think they got good at that?
4. Do you know someone who (mostly) resists the urge to "compare their best with their opponents' worst"? How do you think they acquired that capacity?
5. We say, "When people like each other, the rules change." How do you think that works between people who oppose each other? Have you observed examples of that in your life?
6. If you believed an opponent would listen to you with genuine curiosity, would you be willing to return the favor?

Video interview with Jim Henderson and Jim Hancock: bit.ly/3practices-interview

REFERENCE READING FOR CHAPTER 13:

- "3 Practices for Crossing the Difference Divide" by Jim Henderson and Jim Hancock bit.ly/3practices-book

CHAPTER 11: "TROUBLING THE WATERS: TWO APPROACHES TO CREATING A MORE BEAUTIFUL WORLD" BY REV. BRANDAN ROBERTSON

1. Are you more comfortable working as an advocate or an activist? Why?
2. Not counting LGBTQ+ inclusion, what other issues do you think are better addressed through advocacy? Or through activism?
3. Which should come first, activism or advocacy?
4. How can activism and advocacy work more effectively hand-in-hand?
5. How fully does your community support the LGBTQ+ community?

Video interview with Brandan Robertson: bit.ly/brandan-robertson-interview

REFERENCE READING FOR CHAPTER 11:
- "True Inclusion: Creating Communities of Radical Embrace" – by Brandan Robertson bit.ly/brandan-robertson-book

WEEK 2

CHAPTER 2: "HEALING DIVIDES AS CLOWNING" BY FRANK A. THOMAS

1. Do you know someone who has been cast as a clown in real life? Can you describe the inner strength it takes for this person to persist without bitterness?
2. How do you feel about this person?
3. The author describes "comedic vision" as seeing beauty in all of the ugliness, and says "those who recognize the beauty are called 'fools,' 'holy fools' at that. Fools have a wisdom that discerns beauty in all of the ugliness." Can you name an instance where you have been a "fool" in this way?
4. The author says "The comedic vision allows me to be constructive with my rage. My African American foremothers and forefathers did so many constructive and wonderful things with their rage." The use of comedic vision is one way that the author deals with his rage over racism, and channels that energy to constructive use. What are other ways in which we can channel our rage into constructive use?

5. "The clown is constantly defeated, tricked, humiliated, and trampled upon...Harvey Cox puts it this way, the clown is 'infinitely vulnerable, but never finally defeated.' After falling down, the clown always gets back up." How can we be clowns? Be vulnerable "holy fools" but not defeated?

REFERENCE READING FOR CHAPTER 2:

- "How to Preach a Dangerous Sermon" by Frank A. Thomas bit.ly/frank-thomas-book

CHAPTER 10: "ROOTS OF JUSTICE" BY CALENTHIA DOWDY

1. Have I had a Damascus Road transformative experience? If so, am I willing to share this with others, or do I prefer to reflect on this experience privately?
2. When has my skin color had a positive or negative effect on achieving my goals and dreams?
3. The author mentions "trigger phrases" such as "natural order" and "God's ordained hierarchy" that have been used to justify, among other things, racism. What are some other trigger phrases you've heard?
4. Would your community benefit from the type of antiracism training offered by Roots of Justice? How can you motivate and organize your community to participate?
5. "The knowledge that you and your BIPOC colleagues are not on the same journey and are not having the same or even similar experiences in the same institution can be bewildering. It's difficult to come to grips with the fact that perhaps you're doing so well because you're on a moving sidewalk and your BIPOC colleagues are on an unending jog up many flights of stairs." Have you been on a moving sidewalk or flights of stairs? How can you tell?

CHAPTER 17: "LEARNING TO BE A GOOD RELATIVE: HEARTS AND HANDS" BY SHANNON CROSSBEAR

1. What did you learn about Indigenous people in school? Why do you think you were taught what you were?
2. Do you know the Nations within your State or on whose original homelands you live?
3. Why are Native Americans and Alaskan Natives different from other minority populations within the United States?
4. How might you approach things differently if you knew you were related to a Native American?
5. What does climate action have to do with healing divides?

Video interview with Shannon Crossbear: bit.ly/shannon-crossbear-interview

CHAPTER 19: "THE JULIAN WAY: DISCOVERING THE GIFTS OF DIVERSE EMBODIMENTS WITHIN ALL OF GOD'S PEOPLE" BY JUSTIN HANCOCK

1. In what ways does your group or organizations currently support people with disabilities?
2. The mission of the Summer Institute on Theology and Disability, mentioned in this chapter, is to foster diverse and authentic interfaith conversations at the intersection of theology and disability. You might consider participating in one of the future conferences: https://faithanddisability.org/institute/
3. As with other organizations described in "How to Heal Our Divides" The Julian Way initially used community dinners to foster relationships among abled and disabled individuals. Would that be possible for your organization to do?
4. Did you know that Compassionate Christianity provides links to many resources about disability and faith? You can find them here: https://compassionatechristianity.org/disability-resources/
5. Would you be interested in an accessibility assessment for churches and communities of faith? You can learn more about the service here: https://thejulianway.org/

Video interview with Justin Hancock: bit.ly/justin-hancock-interview

REFERENCE READING FOR CHAPTER 19:
- "Revelations of Divine Love" by Julian of Norwich bit.ly/julian-of-norwich
- "The Julian Way: A Theology of Fullness for All of God's People" by Justin Hancock bit.ly/the-julian-way

WEEK 3

CHAPTER 3: "WHY HEAL OUR DIVIDES? WE NEED TO HEAL OURSELVES" BY DIANA BUTLER BASS

- The author raises the question why? Given the intense degree of polarization we see, should we even try to heal our divides? Why should we try?
- The author mentions a book called The Prince by Niccolò di Bernardo dei Machiavelli who was an Italian diplomat, philosopher, politician, historian and writer who lived during the Renaissance. Today "machiavellian" means "cunning, scheming, and unscrupulous, especially in politics." In addition to casting our votes, what can we do to encourage politicians not to operate that way?
- What are three main causes of division in your community? In our country?
- What actions can I take to begin to achieve solidarity in my community? In my country?
- How will healing public divides also heal ourselves?

REFERENCE READING FOR CHAPTER 3:

- "Freeing Jesus: Rediscovering Jesus as Friend, Teacher, Savior, Lord, Way, and Presence" by Diana Butler Bass bit.ly/diana-butler-bass-book

CHAPTER 15: "A TALE OF TWO BUSES: A VOTE COMMON GOOD STORY" BY VANESSA RYERSE

- For many people, the presidential election of 2016 was a watershed moment that either revealed or deepened the divides in our country. How did it impact you?
- Describe a time when you had a breakthrough in the way you view the world and how that breakthrough has continued to shape your life.
- In what ways have you been using your voice to speak up for what you believe in? In what ways have you not done so yet? What's holding you back?
- The mission of Vote Common Good is to encourage voters to use the common good as their voting criterion rather than what seems good for them personally or for their faith tradition. What might your life look like if the common good was a stronger motivating force for you?
- Where do you see faith, hope, and love being exemplified in American politics? Where do you wish to see them?

Video interview Vanessa Ryerse: bit.ly/vanessa-ryerse-interview

REFERENCE READING FOR CHAPTER 15:

- The Six Values of Common Good Communication bit.ly/six-values-good-communication

CHAPTER 6: "HEALING OUR DIVIDES: PREACHING THE COMMON GOOD" BY MARK FELDMEIR

- Many pastors are reluctant to address potentially divisive issues like those discussed by the author. Should they be? What can you do to help your pastor more easily talk about issues from the pulpit that need to be discussed?
- Quoting the bible: "When I was hungry, thirsty, sick, and in prison, did you care? When I was your neighbor in disguise, your fellow citizen, a stranger, did you love me?" (Matthew 25). The author states: "this is the only kind of politics that mattered to Jesus, and it's the one kind of politics that can inspire people of faith from both sides of the political aisle to find enough common ground to work together for the common good." What can you do to encourage this type of activism in your community?
- "What brought your ancestors to the U.S.? What was their country of origin? When did they arrive and where did they settle?"
- What struggles did your ancestors face in making a new life?

- "The majority of Americans are not on the extremes of any of these issues, but most of what we hear and read is from people who reflect more extreme views. Our natural tendency is to conceptualize everyone on the other side of the political spectrum as though they are representative of the leaders and proponents of that side." How do we help correct these misconceptions?

Video interview with Mark Feldmeir: bit.ly/mark-feldmeir-video

REFERENCE READING FOR CHAPTER 6:
- "A House Divided: Engaging the Issues Through the Politics of Compassion" by Mark Feldmeir:
  bit.ly/mark-feldmeir-book

CHAPTER 9: "HEALING OUR DIVIDES FROM THE INSIDE OUT" BY PARKER J. PALMER

- We humans have forever found ways to make people who are "other" than us into strangers, aliens, or enemies. Where do you think this instinct comes from? Why do we do it?
- Have you known people who engaged in this kind of thinking or acting? Have you ever done it yourself? If so, what purpose did "othering" fulfill in their life or yours?
- Have there been times in your life when you felt a need to hide your "true self" behind a wall? What was going on at that time that made "hiding out" necessary? How did you find your way forward?
- Have you encountered "the stranger within" and found yourself able to embrace that part or parts of yourself? What has been the outcome?
- Based on your experience, what do you suggest to help others get beyond the divisive habit of "othering?" In what setting might you try to lead folks down one or more of these paths toward "the Beloved Community"?

Video interview with Parker Palmer: bit.ly/parker-palmer-interview

REFERENCE READING FOR CHAPTER 9:
- "A Hidden Wholeness: The Journey Toward an Undivided Life" by Parker J. Palmer
  bit.ly/hidden-wholeness
- "Healing the Heart of Democracy: The Courage to Create a Politics Worthy of the Human Spirit" – by Parker J. Palmer bit.ly/heart-of-democracy

WEEK 4

CHAPTER 4: "NOTHING NEW UNDER THE SUN: OPPOSING RACISM TODAY" BY MICHAEL W. WATERS

- If "struggle is a never-ending process" and freedom is never really won," why bother trying to change things?
- Is the call to action strong enough to motivate me to become part of the process of change?
- The author states: "Oftentimes, our divides result from a form of idol worship." What forms of idol worship do you see today?
- "When our god is a manifestation of our unsubstantiated fears and greed, we follow a god shaped and formed exclusively to serve our own callous interests, as opposed to the God who shapes and forms us as a reflection of Godself to care for the concerns of others." What fears do you see that drive people toward their "own callous interests?"
- What can be done to allay these fears?

REFERENCE READING FOR CHAPTER 4:

- "Something in the Water: A 21st Century Civil Rights Odyssey" by Michael W. Waters bit.ly/michael-waters-book

CHAPTER 8: "UNITED IN JOINT MISSION: THE POWER OF RIGHT RELATIONSHIP TO HEAL THE DIVIDES" BY REV. DR. ALEXIA SALVATIERRA

- What does it mean to you to "stand on sacred ground" with someone who is significantly different from you? Have you experienced this? If so, what did you learn? If not, why not?
- Have you ever participated in joint mission (acting on your faith to reach out to and serve others) with someone who is significantly different from you?
- If yes, how was the experience? What did you discover in the process? If not, why not?
- Does providing charity to someone in need change your attitude to them in the same way as working side by side together to accomplish a common goal?
- What do you think causes resistance to working together towards a common goal with someone who is significantly different from your culture or normal networks?
- How can that resistance be overcome?

Video interview with Alexia Salvatierra: bit.ly/alexia-interview

REFERENCE READING FOR CHAPTER 8:

- "Faith-Rooted Organizing: Mobilizing the Church in Service to the World" by Alexia Salvatierra and Peter Heltzel bit.ly/alexia-book

CHAPTER 7: "THE FUTURE OF CHURCH: TRAINING A NEW GENERATION OF LEADERS SEEKING TO BRIDGE THE DIVIDE BETWEEN GOOD INTENTIONS AND LASTING SOCIAL IMPACT" BY RICH TAFEL

- Who is the community outside your church doors that doesn't enter through the doors? What is stopping them?
- How can you package your spiritual, ethical teachings to be accessible to the needs of the younger generation beginning their career?
- What skills do activists in your church or community need to gain to have an impact?
- Who in your church community can provide guidance and what expertise do you need to bring in to help young leaders engage with impact?
- What funds and/or space can you provide to startup spiritual entrepreneurs in your community?

Video interview with Rich Tafel: bit.ly/rich-tafel-interview

CHAPTER 12: "IT BEGINS WITH HUMILITY" BY SHANE CLAIBORNE

- Share an experience where you saw humility open up dialogue or create an opportunity for people with differing viewpoints to find common ground.
- The author gives several examples of protests that expose injustice and amplify the voices of those who are hurting. Can you think of some other examples of creative public actions that you've witnessed?
- What is one organization you're familiar with that is helping to "heal the divides"?
- Is there a specific social issue that you believe is so important that you want to become more actively involved in addressing the issue?
- What can we do to combat self-righteousness in ourselves?

Video interview with Shane Claiborne: bit.ly/shane-interview

REFERENCE READING FOR CHAPTER 12:
- "Jesus for President: Politics for Ordinary Radicals" by Shane Claiborne and Chris Haw bit.ly/shane-book

6 WEEK GROUP DISCUSSION

(WEEKS 1-4 ABOVE)

WEEK 5

CHAPTER 14: "CULTURE CARE" BY MAKO FUJIMURA

- What if each of us endeavored to bring beauty into someone's life today in some small way?
- What if we, by faith, saw each moment as a genesis moment, and even saw the current problems we are facing as genesis opportunities?
- What if we considered our actions, decisions, and creative products in light of five hundred years and multiple generations?
- What if we started to transgress boundaries by integrating our faith, art, and life—and speaking boldly about them?
- What if we committed to speaking fresh creativity and vision into culture rather than denouncing and boycotting other cultural products?
- What if we, like Mahalia Jackson, stood behind our preachers and leaders and exhorted them to "tell 'em about the dream"?
- What if we became custodians of culture, willing to be demoted for standing up for what is right but taking copious notes so we can challenge the status quo?
- What if we assumed that relational and creative capital is infinite? What kind of effect would that have on our business practices?
- Your "What Ifs" - Note down your own what if statements and share them with friends. Consider ways you can use these statements to help birth a plan for your community.

REFERENCE READING FOR CHAPTER 14:
- "Culture Care: Reconnecting with Beauty for Our Common Life" – by Makoto Fujimura bit.ly/mako-book

CHAPTER 18: "BUILDING RECONCILING COMMUNITIES WITH ARRABON" BY DAVID M. BAILEY AND TIFFANIE S. CHAN

- What does "peace-making" mean to you? Please share an instance when you were considered a peace-maker.
- The authors state: "While it may be difficult to recognize in ourselves, it's a sad truth that most Christians are more concerned with being right than with being righteous." Have you seen

other Christians act like this? Have you seen yourself act like this?

- The authors describe one of the key pillars of a reconciling community as "Participate in Cross-Cultural Collaboration." What are examples of cross-cultural collaboration in which your community participates? Are they one-time events or ongoing? Have you been able to develop meaningful relationships with those from the other culture?
- On an individual level, do you have a meaningful relationship with someone from another culture / another race? Does your relationship have a sufficient level of trust to openly discuss racism? How well has that gone?
- The authors talk about going beyond the stages of Awareness and Learning to Sharing, and the benefits of doing this. Please share what you have recently learned from interaction with someone from a different race or culture.

Video interview with David Bailey: bit.ly/david-bailey-interview

REFERENCE READING FOR CHAPTER 18:
- Race, Class, and the Kingdom of God Study Series arrabon.com/study-series/

CHAPTER 21: "FORMING PEACEMAKERS, TRANSFORMING CONFLICT" BY TODD DEATHERAGE

- The primary Telos learning model is through immersive experiences. Have you had some type of intense immersive experience that had an important impact on your life?
- Telos "forms communities of American peacemakers across lines of difference, and equips them to help reconcile seemingly intractable conflicts at home and abroad." What lines of difference exist in your own community, where collaboration might benefit the common good?
- Telos has developed a set of "Principles and Practices of Peacemaking" - which of their principles and which of their practices do you think can have the most impact to lead toward effective peacemaking?
- On their website Telos offers "A Quick Guide to Political Advocacy" (found here: https://www.telosgroup.org/resources/#telos-materials). After reading their suggestions, at what stage of political advocacy do you see yourself?
- Telos trains what they call "Table Hosts" who then guide groups (known as "Telos Tables") through challenging conversations and direct them to real-world impact. Would you be interested in learning more about becoming a Table Host? Here you go: https://www.telosgroup.org/table-hosts/

Video interview with Todd Deatherage: bit.ly/todd-interview
Audio interview with Todd Deatherage and Brian Allain: bit.ly/todd-and-brian-interview

REFERENCE READING FOR CHAPTER 21:

- The Principles and Practices of Peacemaking bit.ly/principles-practices

CHAPTER 26: "CROSSING BOUNDARIES OF FAITH" BY WES GRANBERG-MICHAELSON

- What is the cost and effect of sharp divisions in the global Body of Christ?
- Are religious divisions more difficult to overcome than political ones?
- How have religious divisions impacted you personally? Do you have stories of overcoming them?
- Do you find hope in the story of the Global Christian Forum? Does it inspire you to take any action in your own context?
- Within your local community, are there other religion groups with whom yours could begin to dialogue and potentially collaborate on a project?

Video interview with Wes Granberg-Michaelson: bit.ly/wes-interview

REFERENCE READING FOR CHAPTER 26:

- "Without Oars: Casting Off into a Life of Pilgrimage" by Wes Granberg-Michaelson bit.ly/wes-book

WEEK 6

CHAPTER 16: "AMERICA DOESN'T NEED FEWER ARGUMENTS, IT NEEDS LESS STUPID ONES" BY SETH HENDERSON AND ERIK GROSS

- What historical narratives shaped your childhood view of the world?
- Growing up in the context of corporate America, at least some of us were taught an unwritten rule to never discuss politics, religion, or sex at work. Along with other contributing factors, this has led to our society's inability to discuss such topics effectively. Why do you think they were "banned" in the first place? Do you find these topics difficult to discuss now?
- How do you feel when someone argues against beliefs you deeply value?
- Are you emotionally able to take winning off the table when you believe you are right?
- What can we as individuals do to more readily allow ourselves "more room to transform?"

Video interview with Seth and Erik: bit.ly/seth-erik-interview

REFERENCE READING FOR CHAPTER 16:

- The Better Arguments Resource Library <u>bit.ly/better-arguments</u>

CHAPTER 22: "HEAD, HEART, HANDS: A HOLISTIC RESPONSE TO THE HARMS OF SOCIAL DIVISIONS" BY AMY JULIA BECKER

- What holds you back from participating in social healing?
- What small steps have you taken as an individual to engage in social healing? Has this led to other changes in your life?
- Where do you have influence in your community? How could you use that influence to participate in healing?
- What institutions are you a part of? Do you see areas where those institutions need to change to become more just?
- Are there other people who would join with you to consider those types of changes?
- What action steps do you want to take in response to these ideas?

Video interview with Amy Julia: <u>bit.ly/amy-julia-interview</u>

REFERENCE READING FOR CHAPTER 22:

- "White Picket Fences: Turning Toward Love in a World Divided by Privilege" – by Amy Julia Becker
  <u>bit.ly/amy-julia-book</u>
- "Head, Heart, and Hands: An Action Guide" in .PDF, eBook, and Audiobook formats
  <u>bit.ly/amy-julia-action-guide</u>

CHAPTER 23: "JUST SHOW UP: HOW FOOD AND FAITH BRING PEOPLE TOGETHER" BY MARK CRYDERMAN

- The author reached a point where he recognized he was more concerned about material things such as a house and a yard than he was about ministry. Have you ever felt you were spending too much time, energy, or money on things that really don't matter that much?
- What did the author give up, and what did he gain?
- When it comes to healing divisions between people, the author believes it's important to show up. What does he mean? What are some ways you could "show up" to help heal divisions between people?
- Most people tend to live, socialize, and worship with people who look like them and generally agree with them. How could this contribute to divisions among people?
- The Dinner Church movement uses food to bring people together. What are some other ways your church could bring people together?

- Most churches measure success by the size of their congregation and/or their rate of growth. What are some other metrics for measuring success if healing divisions among people were a priority?

REFERENCE READING FOR CHAPTER 23:
- Dinner Church resources dinnerchurchmovement.org/resources/

CHAPTER 24: "TOWARD A WORLD BEYOND ENEMIES" BY MICHAEL McRAY

- The author describes The Parent Circle, an organization whose members have lost a family member in the Israeli/Palestinian conflict. They find common ground through their shared loss. Can you think of a support group you might want to form, around some other form of loss, that could be either geographically local to you, or geographically dispersed online?
- In Northern Ireland, Corrymeela "welcomes over ten thousand visitors per year, and their calendar of events addresses issues of sectarianism, marginalization, legacies of conflict, and public theology." Could your organization start a local (or online) discussion group around any of these topics?
- "Since 2012, Narrative 4 has facilitated the exchange of over 200,000 stories across 20 countries and half the U.S. states. They are building an expansive network of practitioners and ambassadors for their mission: to increase people's capacity to practice empathy, and then to turn that empathy into action." Would you like to learn more about joining or starting such a group? Visit www.narrative4.com
- Did you know that the chapter's author, Michael McRay, leads retreats: "Becoming Re-Storied: A Weekend Retreat of Story, Self-Exploration, and Empathic Encounter" - you can learn more about them here:
  https://michaelmcray.com/retreats/
- Did you know that Michael also offers several different types of consulting services, including group facilitation and individual coaching in areas such as leadership storytelling for influence, conflict coaching, and mediation? Learn more here:
  https://michaelmcray.com/wp-content/uploads/2021/07/MM-Consulting-Services.pdf

Video interview with Michael McRay: bit.ly/mcray-interview

REFERENCE READING FOR CHAPTER 24:
- "I Am Not Your Enemy: Stories to Transform a Divided World" by Michael McRay bit.ly/mcray-book

8 WEEK GROUP DISCUSSION

(WEEK 1-6 ABOVE)

WEEK 7

CHAPTER 20: "THE COLOSSIAN FORUM: IF THE HOLY SPIRIT DOESN'T SHOW UP, WE'RE SCREWED" BY MICHAEL GULKER

- The author suggests that most churches choose one of two approaches to difficult issues—never talk openly about them, or fight over them until one side "wins." How would you describe your church's experience in resolving serious issues such as LGBTQ inclusion, diversity in leadership, etc.?
- If a person began attending your church whose political views differed from the views held by you and the majority in your congregation, would that person be comfortable and feel welcome? What could you do specifically to make them comfortable?
- The author believes "the Gospel gives us all we need to handle our serious conflicts with grace, even love." If you agree, why do so many churches either try to avoid conflict or split over them, instead of trusting the gospel? If you disagree, explain why.
- How can conflict become an act of worship?
- According to the author, "The problem is that the church is mimicking a divisive culture while proclaiming the Prince of Peace." If the church instead mimicked the Prince of Peace, how might that heal the divisions in culture? How would that church resolve a major issue that was dividing it?
- Do you agree that church is giving us "a theologized version of what they can get on FOX or CNN?" To put it another way, to what extent is media influencing the church?

REFERENCE READING FOR CHAPTER 20:
- Colossian Forum resources: colossianforum.org/projects/books/

CHAPTER 25: "PEACE CATALYST: FOLLOWING JESUS, WAGING PEACE" BY MARTIN BROOKS

- Shalom - What is peace? What is shalom? How would you define or describe it?
- Peacebuilding - When the Bible says to "seek peace and pursue it," what does this mean for you?
- Understanding - Who is "the other" for you or for your community? How can you better understand and empathize with their stories and needs?

- Connecting - Where can you "show up" to connect with others and the work they're already doing? What spaces and work already exist that you can support?
- Collaborating - What are some common goals you can work toward in collaboration with others? What work is already happening that you can support?
- Celebrating - What is one story of a healed relationship that inspires you? How can celebrating such stories help us reimagine what is possible?

Video interview with Martin Brooks: bit.ly/brooks-interview

REFERENCE READING FOR CHAPTER 25:
- "Peace Catalysts" by Rick Love peacecatalyst.org/shop/peace-catalysts-book-1

CHAPTER 27: "HOW TO ADDRESS THE ASYMMETRY OF FAITH AND POLITICS" BY GUTHRIE GRAVES-FITZSIMMONS

- The author raises the issue that "religious" or "Christian" are often mistakenly correlated by the general public to imply "conservative" or "Republican". Have you experienced such generalizations?
- A related misconception is that the Democratic party is "secular". Have you perceived there to be "religious left" or "progressive Christian" groups? What prevents them from being more highly recognized?
- How can religious leaders cooperate "across divides" to work for the common good? How can you aid that in your community?
- The author suggests that we get to know people on "the other side" of issues we care about. (Several other chapter contributors offer the same advice.) What can you do to get to know people on the other side of an issue you care most deeply about?
- The author states that "There are hypocrites and liars in all corners, of course, who use religion as an excuse for advancing their own personal aims." Can you identify instances where you feel that someone on "your side" of an issue did this?

REFERENCE READING:
- "Just Faith: Reclaiming Progressive Christianity" by Guthrie Graves-Fitzsimmons bit.ly/guthrie-book

CHAPTER 28: "HEALING OUR INNER DIVIDES" BY MOLLY LACROIX

- Think of a divide you're navigating. What do you notice inside?
- What emotions, thoughts, sensations, and images emerge?
- Consider connecting with the parts of you holding this information. Are you curious about

them? Would you like to learn more?

- Are you afraid of what it means that you have these thoughts and feelings?
- What if you can reassure the part who is afraid that turning toward all that is provoked by the divide is the way to open your heart?

Video interview with Molly LaCroix: bit.ly/molly-interview

REFERENCE READING FOR CHAPTER 28:

- "Restoring Relationship: Transforming Fear into Love Through Connection" by Molly LaCroix
  bit.ly/molly-book

WEEK 8

CHAPTER 29: "TO CREATE A SHARED FUTURE, SHIFT WHOSE VOICES ARE WELCOME AT THE TABLE" BY K SCARRY

- The People's Supper was formed in the aftermath of the 2016 election. Describe how you felt after that event.
- The methodology used by The People's Supper has been used to address several different types of divides. Brainstorm about what types of divides where you can see this model being useful.
- What serious divides exist in your community that could potentially be helped by this approach?
- The author describes their seminary professor posing the question "What do you think leads toward real change in our communities? Policy change or relationship building?" Please consider and discuss.
- "In racial justice work, make it a series, and offer affinity spaces. Sitting down for one meal together will not do it." What type of ongoing commitment can your organization make to foster relationships that lead to healing?

Video interview with K Scarry: bit.ly/k-scarry-interview

REFERENCE READING FOR CHAPTER 29:

- People's Supper Guidebooks: thepeoplessupper.org/resources

CHAPTER 30: "HOW MORMONISM CAN SAVE AMERICA" BY JANA RIESS

- How can religious organizations be used to "encourage" (force?) each of us out of our own group-think bubbles that only reinforce our existing perceptions?

- How can non-religious organizations do the same?
- "Churches become echo chambers, and those who don't agree with the politics preached from the pulpit become increasingly isolated." Should politics be preached from the pulpit?
- How have you seen political divides play out (or not) within your own faith community?
- "Mormonism teaches me that I don't get to excommunicate folks from my world just because we disagree. And I am so, so glad of it. Being forced out of my comfort zone is – well, uncomfortable. But it's uncomfortable in an important way, as we become better in community with one another than we are when we can pretend the other side is anything less than human." How can we have uncomfortable conversations within our religious communities?

CHAPTER 31: "THREE SHIFTS FOR HEALING RELIGIOUS DIVIDES" BY RABBI RAMI SHAPIRO

- To put it bluntly: while diversity is inherent in nature, divides are narratives one is taught that elevate "the other" as an existential threat to one's privilege, power, and authority. What are some of the narratives you were taught as a child that separated you and your community from others and other communities? How do these narratives continue to play out in your life?
- Religious beliefs are ideas we hold to be true without any evidence outside the religion itself that they are in fact true. What religious beliefs do you hold? How do these beliefs promote division rather than diversity? What leads you to think these beliefs are true? How might you live differently if you knew these beliefs were false?
- Given that there is no objective evidence proving the truth of any religious belief, should we shift from speaking of religious beliefs to religious hypotheses? How would your approach to religion change if you shifted from holding beliefs to testing them as hypotheses?
- At the mystic heart of parochial religion is Perennial Wisdom, a four–fold hypothesis affirmed by the great mystics throughout time and across cultures: 1) All life is the happening of nondual Aliveness called by different names: Brahman, YHVH, Allah, Mother, Tao, Dharmakaya, etc. 2) Human beings have the innate capacity to awaken in, with, and as this Aliveness. 3) Awakening to Aliveness reveals a universal ethic of justice and compassion rooted in the Golden Rule and devoted to the ideal of being a blessing to all the families of the earth, human and otherwise (Genesis 12:3). 4) Awakening to Aliveness and being a blessing comprise the highest calling of every human being. What is your response to the four points of Perennial Wisdom?
- When you shift from belief to hypothesis, you live more humbly. When you shift from metaphysics to metaphor, you think more creatively. When you shift from parochial to the perennial, you free yourself from all divides, seeing self and other—all others—as unique and precious manifestations of an infinite, dynamic, nondual Reality called by many names…This assertion is itself a hypothesis in need of testing. How would you test the veracity of Perennial Wisdom? How would your life change if you discovered it was true?

Video interview with Rabbi Rami: https://bit.ly/rabbi-rami-interview

REFERENCE READING FOR CHAPTER 31:

- "Perennial Wisdom for the Spiritually Independent: Sacred Teachings" by Rabbi Rami bit.ly/rabbi-rami-book

CHAPTER 32: "THE PEACE PATH MODEL: BRIDGING THE MUSLIM/CHRISTIAN DIVIDE" BY JEFF BURNS

- The author describes himself as an "Evangelical Islamophobic Minister" before he met a little Muslim boy named Omar. He viewed Muslims as "intrinsically evil people." Can you identify on any level with his struggle with Islamophobia? Perhaps your struggle is with another group. Can you share a little of that struggle with your group?
- The author considers his encounter with Omar a second conversion. Why? Because he prayed for a sign and within a couple of minutes Omar, the five-year-old Muslim boy, appeared! What were the key elements of his experience with little Omar that led to his change of heart towards Muslims?
- The author says that the core theological message of Jesus is the foundation of the PP Model. What is Jesus' core message? Why is this core message effective in helping Muslims and Christians find common theological ground to build a peaceful bridge between faith communities?
- The author believes that the core message is only a noble idea unless certain practices contextualize it. The PP model is based upon Five Practices. What are those practices, and why are they so effective in building community between Muslims and Christians? How do the Five Practices connect with the Dream and Mission of God?
- The author gives two examples of Muslim and Christian practitioners who are using the PP model. Comment on your observations of how the practitioners' stories are similar and different. Why do you believe they both seem to like and benefit from the model, even though they are from two other religions?

Video interview with Jeff Burns: bit.ly/jeff-burns-interview

REFERENCE READING FOR CHAPTER 32:

- Free Peacemaking Ecourse: jeffburns.org/peace-path-model/

CHAPTER 33: "HERE I RAISE MY EBENEZER" BY ADAM THOMAS

- Which of the chapters in this book spoke most closely to the intersection of where your deep gladness meets the world's deep hunger? What about that chapter spoke to you and what is it spurring you to do now?
- Share a story about a time you learned a new word or concept that helped open up a new realm

of experience.

- What common words and phrases like "violence against women" and "slave" reinforce unjust systems in our society? What words and phrases can we replace them with to help dismantle those systems?

- Which large category of our divides (political, racial, religious, etc.) do you feel most passionately about healing? What personal experiences have led you to that passion?

- As you think about healing divides, what holds you back? How can you ask others for help in order to open yourself enough to step into the work of healing?

- What commitments are you ready to make or renew in order to partner with God as a force for healing and reconciliation in the world?

NOTES

NOTES

NOTES